Putting on the Brakes

Understanding and **Taking Control** of Your **ADD** or **ADHD**

3rd Edition

By Patricia O. Quinn, MD
and Judith M. Stern, MA

MAGINATION PRESS•WASHINGTON, DC
American Psychological Association

To my grandkids: Caroline, Frannie, Anna, Georgia,
Fiona, Tommy, Bobby, and Catie Quinn —*POQ*

To Uzi, Tali, Naomi and Emma —*JMS*

Published by
MAGINATION PRESS
An Educational Publishing Foundation Book
American Psychological Association
750 First Street, NE
Washington, DC 20002

For more information about our books, including a complete catalog, please write to us, call 1-800-374-2721, or visit our website at http://www.apa.org/pubs/magination/

Printed by Worzalla, Stevens Point, Wisconsin

Book design and doodles by Sandra Kimbell

Cover photo by Ryan McVay/Photodisc/Getty Images

Photographs appearing on page 17, 66, 80, 84 by Hemera Technologies/Able Stock.com/Getty Images; page 22, 34, 36, 44, 48, 50, 54, 86 by Jupiterimages/liquidlibrary/Getty Images; page 24, 27, 52, 65, 67, 96 by Jupiterimages/Photos.com/Getty Images; page 14 by Glowimages/Glowimages/Getty Images; page 61 by Hemera Technologies/Photos.com/Getty Images; page 89 by Photos.com; page 37 by George Doyle/Stockbyte/Getty Images; page 40 by Stockbyte/Stockbyte/Getty Images; page 13, 39 by Sandra Kimbell.

Library of Congress Cataloging-in-Publication Data
Quinn, Patricia O.
   Putting on the brakes : understanding and taking control of your ADD or ADHD / by Patricia O. Quinn and Judith M. Stern.—3rd ed.
      p. cm.
   Summary: "Self-help guide and resource for preteens with attention deficit disorder (ADD) or attention deficit-hyperactivity disorder (ADHD). Includes strategies to manage the disorder and practical ways to improve organization, focus, studying, and homework skills. Also tips for making friends, controlling emotions, and being healthy"—Provided by publisher.
   Includes bibliographical references.
   ISBN 978-1-4338-1134-0 (pbk. : alk. paper)—ISBN 978-1-4338-1135-7 (hardback : alk. paper)
   1. Attention-deficit hyperactivity disorder—Juvenile literature. I. Stern, Judith M. II. Title.
   RJ506.H9Q5482 2012
   616.85'89—dc23

10 9 8 7 6 5 4 3 2

Contents

About This 20th Anniversary Edition

Twenty years! As with any anniversary, our first response to hearing that *Putting on the Brakes* was first published 20 years ago was, "It seems like only yesterday!"

Almost immediately, we thought of the hundreds of thousands of boys and girls who read the first *Putting on the Brakes* in the early 1990s. They would be grown-ups by now and might even have children of their own. We thought of the hundreds of kids and parents who have written to us over the years to tell us about their experiences with *Putting on the Brakes*, like the mother who was talking to her son about his misbehavior, and he asked her to get "that" book. "What book?" she asked. Her son replied, "That *Putting on the Brakes* book that says I'm as smart and capable as other kids." Or the fourth grader who stood up in class to do his oral book report on our book and declared proudly, "I have ADD and am learning to put on the brakes!" Or a counselor from a children's clinic who told us that this was the book they gave to all children newly diagnosed with AD/HD in their community. We fondly call these our *Putting on the Brakes* stories.

We also thought of children all over the world who now have more information on AD/HD as *Putting on the Brakes* has been translated into Spanish, Japanese, Polish, Finnish, Hebrew, Portuguese, Chinese, and Arabic.

We thought of the struggles we had getting *Putting on the Brakes* published in the first place. In 1990, no non-fiction book existed to educate kids with AD/HD about their disorder and how they could deal with it in a positive way. Publishers suggested that we write a fiction book about the life of a boy with AD/HD instead. That was not our aim. We each worked with children with AD/HD every day, and knew them well. We wanted to empower children with AD/HD, including girls who were often overlooked and under-diagnosed at the time. We firmly believed that kids deserved a realistic book that spoke directly to them in language they could understand. The publication of the original *Putting on the Brakes* by Brunner/Mazel Publishers was certainly a professional highlight for each of us, especially as we heard great things from parents who had used the book and professionals from all over the country who kept copies in their offices to share with families.

Many things have changed over the last 20 years. Magination Press (an imprint of the American Psychological Association) acquired the title and through the years encouraged us to keep the book up-to-date as AD/HD developed into a better-understood disorder. Other things have changed as well, particularly with respect to the diagnosis and treatment of AD/HD. More children than ever are being diagnosed. The last Centers for Disease Control report from 2007 indicates that, according to their parents, 9.5 percent of all children have had an AD/HD diagnosis. That represents approximately 5.4 million children. Newer long-acting medications (both stimulants and non-stimulants) are now available to treat AD/HD. Teachers are better trained to recognize the impact of AD/HD on children in the classroom and to provide effective intervention. Counselors and therapists who treat children with AD/HD are able to provide important services to them and their parents. Coaching and other cognitive–behavioral therapies have been introduced as treatments for AD/HD.

However, as we think back through all this, we realize that much remains the same. Kids still need to learn about their AD/HD, how it affects them, and what they can do to take control of their symptoms, emotions, and academic performance to ensure success. Kids need straightforward explanations and reassurance that AD/HD can be managed. Kids need to know that they are not alone. Kids with AD/HD are the reason we wrote this book in the first place and they continue to motivate us to share what we have learned over the past 20 years.

It is with great pride that we welcome you to this new "20th anniversary" edition of *Putting on the Brakes*.

Patricia O. Quinn, MD
Judith M. Stern, MA

How to Use This Book

When kids learn they have an attention disorder, they often need help understanding what that means. Over the years, we have heard their questions (and yours), as well as the doubt, confusion, and fear that sometimes accompany the diagnosis. Together, we, a pediatrician and an educator, wrote this book to answer a wide range of questions, offer encouragement and reassurance, and provide our readers with kid-friendly solutions and tools for taking control of their AD/HD.

Putting on the Brakes may be used in different ways depending on your child's age and reading ability. Your child may be able to read this book on his or her own and then discuss concepts or questions with you. However, many parents find that reading this book together, or reading it to their child, creates an opportunity for ongoing discussion and exploration of the book's content. We have carefully used concepts and vocabulary appropriate to readers ages 8–13, providing them with realistic information that they can use in their everyday lives. This book is set up so that it can be read in smaller sections or used as a reference for handling specific situations or to deal with issues that arise. Kids should be encouraged to read this book a number of times, as they may absorb additional meaning each time.

By introducing your child to *Putting on the Brakes*, you have taken a significant step in providing him or her with the support and reassurance needed to successfully manage AD/HD. As you and your child use this book, some words or concepts may need additional explanation. Giving extra examples, or discussing personal experiences, will allow you to make the information more relevant for your child. Taking time to correct misunderstandings, share insights, or answer questions that arise can be critical to fostering a better understanding of AD/HD. The Resources section at the end of the book has additional materials that you may find helpful. You might also encourage your child to look up unfamiliar words in the glossary of the book.

Kids are capable of dealing with many of their struggles themselves and come to understand that they can be a powerful force in improving their lives. *Putting on the Brakes* attempts to assist kids in not only understanding their AD/HD, but also gaining a sense of control. We have placed a special emphasis on empowering our readers and strived to provide ideas and techniques for kids to use to help themselves. In addition, kids with AD/HD are reassured that parents, teachers, counselors, and other adults are there to help them when they need it. We want kids to know that they are not alone! We also want them to know that millions of kids (and grown-ups) have AD/HD. The problems our readers encounter are not unique. We hope our readers find comfort in knowing that many children and adults have successfully found ways to manage AD/HD.

Along with learning coping skills, we encourage our readers to appreciate their strengths. Kids with AD/HD are smart and capable, and are more like other kids than they may realize.

Teachers, physicians, and mental health professionals may find this book and its companion activity books (*The Putting on the Brakes Activity Book for Kids with ADD or ADHD* and *50 Activities and Games for Kids with ADHD*) useful in helping children better understand AD/HD and adopt strategies to deal with it. These books may also be used by professionals when working with a small group of children who are engaged in the process of learning about their attention disorder.

This book is not meant to replace professional consultation and treatments, which should be part of an ongoing process in the lives of children diagnosed with AD/HD.

Understanding AD/HD is a complex task. However, beginning the process will open up a world of positive possibilities for the child with AD/HD.

PART 1

Understanding AD/HD

CHAPTER 1

AD/HD: What Is It?

Imagine a sleek, red sports car driving around a track. It's flying down the stretches, speeding around the curves, smooth and low to the road, the engine racing...BUT...

it has no brakes. It can't stop when the driver wants it to stop. It can't slow down to a safer speed. It may get off the track or even crash! It will certainly have a hard time proving to everyone what it really can do.

If you have an attention deficit disorder, you may be like that racing car. You have a good engine (with lots of thinking power) and a good strong body, but your brakes don't always work very well. You might not be able to keep still, stay focused, or stop yourself from doing something, even when you know you should stop.

14

What Is AD/HD?

Not everyone with an attention disorder is exactly the same. A person with AD/HD may have any or all of the following problems:

- Trouble paying attention
- Trouble focusing on just one thing at a time
- Trouble keeping still
- Trouble thinking before acting
- Trouble keeping track of things
- Trouble learning in school

Experts who work with kids with attention disorders have named three different types of AD/HD, depending on which problems are causing the most trouble. That is why some kids have ADD (or **Attention Deficit Disorder**) while others have ADHD (or **Attention Deficit Hyperactivity Disorder**). They simply have different problems.

Not everyone with an attention disorder is exactly the same.

✱ One type of attention disorder is called **Inattentive Type** and describes kids who mainly have difficulty paying attention (inattention) and staying focused (distractibility).

15

✱ Another type is called **Hyperactive/Impulsive Type** and includes kids who have more difficulty with keeping still when they need to (hyperactivity) and who frequently act before they think things through (impulsivity).

✱ And finally, many kids with attention disorders have a combination of all of these problems. So, there is a third type called **Combined Type.**

You have probably seen and heard different names and initials used to describe different types of attention problems. ADD and ADHD are the most common names used. In this book, we will usually use the term **AD/HD** to include all three types. *No matter which of the types describes you, this book will help you better understand and take control of your AD/HD.*

The following pages describe some of the problems that young people with AD/HD may face. As you are reading, see if any of these problems sound familiar to you.

Inattention (Trouble Paying Attention)

If you have trouble staying tuned in or paying attention to one thing for more than a few minutes, you may have a short attention span. This is called **inattention.** If you only have problems in this area and are not hyperactive, you have "Attention Deficit Disorder–Inattentive Type." A deficit means that there is less of something than is needed.

Having difficulty paying attention may affect you at home or school with friends. Problems with attention may cause you to:

- Take longer to start or finish assignments or chores.
- Miss directions and not know what to do.
- Not hear what is being said in class or when talking with your friends.

We all find it easier to **concentrate** when we are interested in something, so paying attention may be easier when you are doing something you like. It may be much easier to pay attention when the subject interests you than when the topic is difficult or uninteresting. Your parents and teachers may be confused by this and might think you should be able to pay attention all the time. You may get angry when an adult keeps telling you to pay attention, especially when you feel that you are trying very hard to do just that. Even when you try, the results may not be as good as you (or your parents or teachers) expect. You may need to talk with your parents or teachers and let them know that you *are* trying, but it is difficult for you to concentrate.

Distractibility (Trouble Focusing on One Thing)

Kids with AD/HD have more trouble than others focusing on just one thing. Unrelated ideas, sights, and sounds keep interrupting their focus or thoughts. This is called **distractibility.**

When you are taking a math test, thoughts about a ball game, lunch, or another activity may keep you from concentrating on the test. It may be hard to listen to your teacher when you find so many other things to look at or listen to in the classroom. You may be playing with the pencil on your desk or watching the man mowing the lawn outside instead of focusing on the lesson. A bird singing outside the window or someone walking near you may keep you from hearing the teacher give an assignment.

Kids say that having AD/HD feels like constantly switching channels on a TV. Their brains are just not able to stay tuned in to one channel. Because of difficulties staying focused, you sometimes miss what is going on around you. When many different thoughts keep popping into your head, one right after the other, they interfere with what you are trying to do.

Hyperactivity (Trouble Keeping Still)

If you are **hyperactive,** it may be difficult for you to keep still. You find that you always have to be moving. Sitting in one place is especially hard and may make you feel very restless. You definitely feel better when you can stand up, fidget, or move around. Not being able to move may make you feel upset, anxious, tired, or sleepy. Some hyperactive kids talk too much, without giving others a turn.

It is frustrating to be told over and over to stop moving or stop talking. Like the racecar that doesn't have any brakes, you may have difficulty stopping even when you want to stop.

Impulsivity (Trouble Thinking before Acting)

Sometimes you may do or say things without thinking. You may ride your bicycle through your parents' garden, or call out the answer in class without raising your hand, or start a test before you've heard all the directions. You may interrupt others or say the first thing that comes into your head, whatever that is!

Doing or saying something without thinking—because you don't have brakes to stop you—is called **impulsive behavior** or **impulsivity.** People may ask, "Why did you do that?" At that moment, you may not know, so you'll say, "I don't know." Afterwards, you may be able to discuss what you did wrong. However, you may still forget to "think before you act" the next time. This can be very frustrating for you and the people around you.

> Sometimes you may do or say things without thinking.

Disorganization
(Trouble Keeping Track of Things)

Kids with AD/HD can be **disorganized.** If you are disorganized, you may have problems keeping track of belongings, school assignments, due dates, or chores. You may forget or lose things more than other kids. You may not know how to keep track of time or how to manage it well. In the morning, you may suddenly discover you have run out of time and that the school bus has arrived, and you are still not ready. You may forget assignments or not have the correct books at home to complete your homework. As a result, your homework may be late. Or you may postpone school assignments until the last minute and then have to rush to get them done. The work you turn in may not show all you really know. When you get these assignments back with lots of corrections, you may be disappointed knowing that you could have done better if you had started earlier.

Learning Difficulties and Learning Disabilities (Trouble Learning in School)

Because of these problems, kids with AD/HD may have trouble in school. Sometimes, they have more difficulty with reading, writing, or math than other students. If this sounds like you, you may have **learning difficulties** along with your AD/HD. You may need a **tutor** or a coach to keep you **organized** or help you with your work, but you are just as smart as other kids.

Some kids with AD/HD may also have a **learning disability** in certain subject areas, such as reading, math, or writing. This means that they are learning, but at a level that is below what is expected for their intelligence and grade level. You could have a learning disability in one subject, and do very well in other school subjects. Or you may have trouble in several subjects. When these difficulties or disabilities are combined with AD/HD, school may sometimes feel especially hard. If

a child with AD/HD has a learning disability, he or she may work with a **learning specialist** to make progress in the subject or subjects that are causing trouble. Teachers know many ways to work with students who have learning problems and can give extra support so students can do a better job in their classes.

Why Am I Like This?

As you read more of this book and learn about AD/HD, you'll be surprised to find out many new things about yourself. First, know that you are not alone! Millions of kids (and grown-ups) have AD/HD. The problems you face are the same as lots of other kids, too. Many kids and adults have successfully found ways to manage their AD/HD. Along with learning some new coping skills, we hope you will begin to appreciate your strengths, too. Appreciating who you are helps a great deal. You have a lot of strengths. There are many positive things to say about you! Kids with AD/HD are smart and capable, and are more like other kids than they often realize. And just like other kids, most kids with AD/HD have lots of questions. Have you ever asked yourself,

How do I know if I really have AD/HD?

Who can have AD/HD?

What is going on in my brain?

Why do I feel this way?

In this book, we will try to answer these questions.

CHAPTER 2

How Do You Know
If You Have AD/HD?

Everyone has some of the problems we talked about in the last chapter, some of the time. It can be hard to pay attention in school when you are thinking about your birthday party tomorrow or your new baby sister. Sometimes when kids are going through a tough time at home, like when someone is sick or a relative has died, worry or sadness may make them restless, irritable, forgetful, or they may have trouble paying attention. But does this mean that they have AD/HD?

If you have had attention problems for a long time and they are not related to a **stressful** situation, you may have AD/HD. Only **professionals** who are experts in how children develop can decide if you have AD/HD. These experts include: **pediatricians, psychologists, psychiatrists, neurologists,** and other professionals, who know all about AD/HD and can help kids who have it.

Sometimes you need to visit more than one specialist. During these visits, the specialist **evaluates** how you learn and your ability to concentrate. The **evaluation** may take several hours. The experts will also talk to your parents and teachers. They might have teachers and parents fill out forms that describe your behavior, attention, and learning ability. After gathering all this information, the experts will decide whether or not you have one of the three types of AD/HD that we talked about on pages 15 and 16.

CHAPTER 3

Who Can Have AD/HD?

Can you guess who in this class has AD/HD? You can't tell, because kids with AD/HD look just like everybody else!

About 1 in every 10 kids has a problem with attention that affects his or her learning or behavior. As many as 5.4 million school-age kids in the United States may have AD/HD. A class

of 20–30 students might have 2 or 3 kids with some type of AD/HD. Both boys and girls have AD/HD. We also know that kids all around the world have AD/HD. Did you know this book has been translated into many languages so that AD/HD kids from around the world can learn about themselves, too?

People used to think that kids with AD/HD were easy to spot because of their hyperactivity. But we now know that many kids have AD/HD (Inattentive Type) and are not hyperactive, so they may be more difficult to identify.

Although you may feel different from kids who don't have AD/HD, you are not alone. You have lots of company when you consider how many other kids your age have AD/HD!

AD/HD in Boys and Girls

Some people think that only boys can have AD/HD. Wrong! Girls can have AD/HD, too. Both boys and girls with AD/HD may have trouble sitting still and may fidget a lot. However, girls with AD/HD usually have more problems with *inattention* than *hyperactivity*. When girls are hyperactive, they may talk a lot or have out-of-control emotions. Whatever their symptoms, girls with AD/HD have just as many problems at school and at home as boys with AD/HD.

AD/HD in Your Family

AD/HD can be **inherited,** so you might find that there are other people in your family with the same or similar problems. You may want to talk to some of these relatives about your AD/HD, because they will have experience in dealing with AD/HD and can understand how you feel.

CHAPTER 4

What Is Going on in the AD/HD Brain?

The **brain** is made up of several areas, each with its own specific job. The outside layers of the brain are called the **cerebral cortex.** This is the part of the brain where most thinking and learning takes place. It is also where memories are stored.

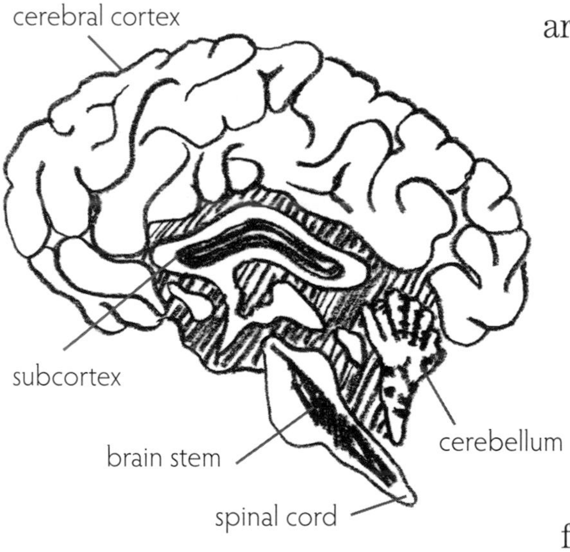

Under the cortex is an area called the **subcortex.** The subcortex helps you stay alert and coordinates your brain's activities. It contains the relay system, which has many jobs. The **relay system** takes information coming in from your senses (like hearing, sight, touch) and

cerebral cortex

subcortex

brain stem

spinal cord

cerebellum

decides where it should go in the cortex. It determines what to pay attention to, and sends messages to "turn on" other parts of your brain, including the braking or inhibiting system. The center for your emotions (anger, fear, happiness, or excitement) and the reward center (an area that becomes active when something gives you pleasure or makes you happy) are also in this layer. That probably explains why you can pay better attention when you like a certain activity or when you know you will receive a reward when you finish.

The brain is made up of many cells called **neurons.** These cells work together, but do not actually touch each other. They are separated by a tiny space called a **synapse.** The neurons send information or messages to each other by sending a chemical messenger across this space. These messengers are called **neurotransmitters.**

For the neuron to relay the message to the cells around it, there must be enough of the neurotransmitter (messenger) to do the job, and the messenger must stay in the synapse (space) long enough to join with a receptor on each of the surrounding cells. This joining of the neurotransmitter to the receptor is like a key fitting into a lock. When the neurotransmitter (*key*) fits into the receptor (*lock*), it opens the door for messages to get through.

When the brain is working properly, there is enough of the neurotransmitter to turn on the cells and deliver the messages where they are supposed to go. If a person has AD/HD, this may not always be happening. Messages to put on the brakes, to slow down, and to pay attention may not be getting through, and that person may then act without thinking (**impulsivity**) or be very distracted by other things going on (**distractibility**).

Scientists have several explanations for why messages are poorly transmitted (*sent*) when someone has

AD/HD. When scientists took **scans** (*pictures*) of the brain in people with AD/HD, they found that the areas that control attention and help with planning were not working properly or developed more slowly. When this happens, there is not enough of the neurotransmitter to turn on the neurons in these areas and keep them turned on so that they can do their job.

Scientists have found that there is a system of proteins in each cell that takes the neurotransmitter from the synapse and carries it back inside the neuron (*cell*) that first sent it out. These proteins are called transporters and make up a **transporter system** at the edge of the cell. It seems that some people with AD/HD have too many of these transporters (*proteins*). This causes the neurotransmitter to be taken back into the cell before it can relay the message to nearby cells. When this happens, other areas of the brain cannot do their job. This helps explain why kids with AD/HD have trouble paying attention, putting on the brakes, getting organized, and why they may forget or lose things.

Scientists know that while problems with neurotransmitters affect some of the brain's jobs, like learning and remembering, they do not affect intelligence, personality, or creativity. Kids with AD/HD are just as smart, talented, and healthy as other kids.

CHAPTER 5

How Does AD/HD
Make You Feel?

If you have AD/HD you may have lots of different thoughts and feelings. Sometimes you feel:

Confused   Impatient   Dumb

Overloaded   Restless   Scared

Angry   Frustrated

Misunderstood   Impulsive   Teased   Tense

Anxious   Picked on

Unpopular   Lost   Forgetful

Let's look at some causes of these feelings.

✱ **Confused or lost.** You may feel confused or lost if you tune out and miss important pieces of information. Even if you look and listen carefully, some of the information just never seems to get to where it needs to go in your brain.

* **Overloaded.** You may feel overloaded if too much information comes in at one time. You may also feel this way when you can't keep up with your assignments, hand work in on time, or finish your work.

* **Restless.** You may feel restless when you have to sit still or when a task is boring.

* **Impatient.** You may feel impatient and have a hard time waiting. You may call out answers in class or have trouble waiting your turn in a game.

* **Impulsive.** If you are impulsive, you may start things before you fully understand what to do. You may rush through assignments at school without checking them afterward and make careless errors.

* **Frustrated or angry.** You may feel frustrated and angry because you really knew the right answer, but your grades don't show it.

* **Forgetful or dumb.** You may find it hard to study and take tests. Even when you review the material ahead of time, the information

33

somehow "disappears" by the time the test begins. Then you may feel forgetful and dumb.

✳ **Scared, anxious, or tense.** You may feel scared or anxious when you know you have a test coming up. When you feel tense, it is even harder for you to pay attention.

✳ **Picked on.** You may feel picked on if your parents scold or nag you more than they do your brothers or sisters. You may need more reminders than other family members because your impulsive behaviors may sometimes be unsafe. Your parents care about your safety and happiness. They try to help you do what is best for you, but you may sometimes feel like you are always being told what to do.

✳ **Unpopular, misunderstood, or teased.** You may feel unpopular or think you don't have any friends. If you often say or do things before you think, other kids might not want to be with you. If you cannot wait

34

your turn or follow the rules during games, other kids may not want to be your friend. If you are messy or can't sit still, you may be teased. All this can make you feel misunderstood.

Now for the good news!

Kids with AD/HD are just as smart as other kids. Having attention deficits does not affect your intelligence! Kids with AD/HD also have lots of positive feelings and skills. You may be:

Energetic Funny Curious Athletic
Special Creative Artistic Sensitive
Humorous Attractive Smart Imaginative
Enthusiastic Friendly Caring Happy

What are you good at? Can you list some of your positive qualities?

There are also good things that come with having AD/HD. You might be:

● **Energetic and enthusiastic.** You can use your extra energy and enthusiasm in many positive ways.

- **Athletic.** You may love to run and jump, play sports, or dance. You may be very athletic, and people look up to you for those talents.

- **Creative and imaginative.** You may be very creative and have many good ideas. Your **curiosity** and imagination may help you think and do things in ways that other people may truly admire. You may be **artistic,** too.

- **Humorous and funny.** You may have a good sense of humor and make other people laugh.

- **Sensitive and caring.** You may be especially sensitive and caring and very aware of other people's feelings.

- **Helpful and friendly!** You may like to help people and be extremely friendly.

And, of course, kids with AD/HD are as attractive, smart, special, and as happy as anyone else.

Ready for some more good news?

Because you have had to deal with the problems of AD/HD from an early age, you have learned many things about yourself. You have the advantage of knowing your strengths and weaknesses. You know how to work hard to solve problems and accomplish your goals. You should be very proud of yourself!

Now that you have learned more about AD/HD, the next part of this book will tell you some ways that you can put on the brakes and feel more in control of your life.

PART 2

Taking Control
of AD/HD

CHAPTER 6

Managing AD/HD

If you have AD/HD, many things can help make life easier. Managing AD/HD takes teamwork. While you can take some of the steps to control your AD/HD by yourself, there are also many people who can help you.

In the following chapters we will talk about how you and your parents, teachers, doctors, and other professionals can work together to treat your AD/HD.

To manage your AD/HD, you may need to learn new ways to interact with others. You may want to try tools to control your behaviors and improve your schoolwork. The specialists you see will recommend different ways to treat your AD/HD. Some specialists may prescribe medication to improve attention and decrease hyperactivity. You may talk with a counselor or **therapist.** You may work with a **resource teacher** or **learning specialist** in school or a **tutor** outside of school.

YOU can help by taking good care of yourself, getting plenty of exercise, and choosing healthy foods to eat. You can learn new ways to control your anger and reduce your stress. Teachers can help you learn new ways to become organized and improve your work and focus in class.

See, there *is* lots of good news. Once you know you have AD/HD, you and your team can get to work to make a positive difference in your life.

41

CHAPTER 7

Building a Support Team

We all need people in our lives who are able to see what is special about us and give us help when things feel hard. Kids with AD/HD need support like everyone else. It is important to know that you don't need to manage everything alone. There are many ways to get extra help.

Your Support Team

Here is a list of some of the people who can help and support you if you have AD/HD:

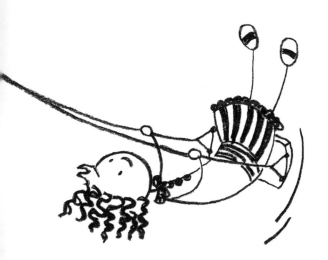

- Parents
- Family
- Guidance Counselor
- Group
- Grandparents
- Therapist
- Friends
- Teacher
- Doctor

Here are some ways kids with AD/HD have found support:

"My parents help me out by listening to my problems and working on homework with me."

"I call my grandmother once a week. She is happy to hear about all the good things I've done and gives helpful advice when I have a problem."

"I meet with a therapist to talk about my feelings and to get some ideas for solving problems that bother me."

"Outside of school, I go to a group with other kids. We work with a counselor who helps us understand our problems and feel good about ourselves. Sometimes the counselor also works with our families to learn new ways to help us."

"I meet with my teacher at school several times a month to talk, get extra help with my work, and find out if I'm missing any assignments."

"My doctor helps me. She prescribes medication to help me concentrate and pay attention."

"I go to the guidance counselor at school when I need to talk about problems I'm having or how I'm feeling."

When you have AD/HD, getting a little extra help can make a big difference. If you look around, you will see that there are many people who can give you the help you need. Depending on what you need, your support "team" might include: your parents, teachers, counselor, tutor, **AD/HD coach**, speech/language teacher, therapist, and your doctor.

Members of your family are a very important part of your support team. Parents can work with you to solve many different problems. They can make homework suggestions, provide ideas for getting organized, and come up with ways to help you improve your ability to focus. If something is bothering you, discussing it with a parent or other relative may give them the information they need to help you. This can be a good way to let your parents know how you would like them to help you.

Your classroom teachers work with you every day, so they have a good understanding about how you learn and get along with your classmates. Set up special times to talk with your teacher in private. Together you can come up with a plan to help you complete all of your classwork and homework.

Resource teachers, or learning specialists, tutors, and coaches work with many students who have attention problems. They can provide suggestions for improving

When you have AD/HD, getting a little extra help can make a big difference.

organization skills, keeping up with homework, and learning how to follow directions. Since they sometimes work with you alone or in a small group, they really get to know you and can help figure out strategies to help you.

School counselors may meet with your parents or teachers to provide them with ideas to use at home or school. Some kids with AD/HD meet with a counselor to learn how to get along better with others and to make friends.

Kids with AD/HD may also meet with a **therapist** (a **psychologist, counselor,** or **social worker**) outside of school to better understand themselves and find ways to solve problems.

Talking with a therapist gives you an opportunity to explore the different feelings you have. A therapist can offer suggestions to help you improve in areas such as learning to control your anger, making friends, getting along with your family, and finding ways to deal with teasing. The therapist may work with you to help you manage problems that come along with your AD/HD, so that you become more organized and in control. He or she may meet with your parents to give them suggestions for helping you at home and school.

When you talk to your therapist, you can be totally honest and say what you think. When you talk about what bothers you or what you wish could happen, the therapist will help guide you in setting up a plan for success. The therapist is on your side, and ready to help make things feel a little easier for you.

You really are the most important part of this team.

Your doctor is another important member of your team. He or she will make sure you are healthy and, if you need it, can prescribe medication to help with your AD/HD symptoms. Visit your doctor regularly for check-ups and tell him or her how you are feeling. Be sure to report any negative side effects of your medications or other problems that you are having.

Everyone on your team will work hard to make you feel great, but you really are the most important part of this team. Your ideas, cooperation, and hard work all add up when it comes to making things better.

CHAPTER 8

Working Together
to Manage Your Behaviors

By working as a team, you, your parents, teachers, and other professionals can create a program to manage your AD/HD, and help you to feel more in control.

Along with learning to keep your cool and handle your anger and frustration (see Chapter 10), it is important to manage your behaviors at home. Holding regular family meetings will help you find solutions to problems. These meetings allow all family members to have an equal say, to learn how to negotiate (have a discussion with someone so that you come to an agreement), and make decisions that everyone accepts. With practice, you'll soon have fewer problems and get along well with your family. You can also use these skills to help you get along better with friends.

Here are some other ideas to think about.

Help Your Parents Help You

Ask adults to let you know when they see you handle a situation well or when you stay in control. And, when your parents say something that is helpful to you, be sure to let them know so they will remember to do it again!

Learn from Your Mistakes

Mistakes often teach us what to do differently next time. For example, if you leave your bike outside (even

though the rule is to put it away), rain may cause it to rust or it might get stolen. This is a negative consequence of your behavior. Talk with your parents about situations that ended badly and identify the behavior and its consequences. Then discuss what you would do differently next time. Now you've learned from your mistake.

Ask Questions

Sometimes your parents may ignore you or get angry and you might have difficulty figuring out why. Maybe they asked you to sit still, and you were fidgety. Or maybe you forgot to clean out your backpack or to do some of your homework. To find out, talk to them. Ask them if you did something that upset them. They may be able to give you pointers for changing your behavior or talk about how they would like you to behave in the future. It is important to talk to your parents and find out what they think about a behavior. This shows that you are interested in being responsible for your behavior.

Set up a System of Rewards

Work with your parents and teachers to set up a system of rewards for your positive behaviors and consequences for when you break the rules. This works best when you focus on one or two behaviors at a time. Ask what specific behaviors these adults are looking for. Then, you will be more likely to earn a reward. Try to find rewards that excite you and make sure your parents agree to those rewards. Perhaps you can earn tickets, tokens, or points for good behaviors.

Take a Time-Out

You have probably heard about "time-out." Maybe you have even spent time there. Most kids think of time-out as a punishment. However, it is really meant to be a place where

you can go to get yourself together and think about your behavior. It gives you a chance to calm down so you can go back to what you were doing and complete it. You might even consider taking your own time-out when you need to gain control over your behavior and avoid getting in trouble in the first place.

As you get older, you may create your own form of time-out. Some kids go to a special, quiet place when they need to get away or calm down. Listening to music, reading a book, or taking a walk may also help create a good feeling of time-out for you.

CHAPTER 9

Being a Good Friend

Now that you have learned more about AD/HD and have begun to understand yourself better, this may be a good time to work on making and keeping friends. Having friends makes everybody feel good! For some kids with AD/HD, making friends or being part of a group can be difficult. If you always want things your way, have trouble waiting your turn, don't listen, or say and do things without thinking, other kids may not want to be your friend. But with some extra work, you can learn how to be a good friend.

What Makes a Good Friend?

Let's think about what makes someone a good friend. A friend:

- Shares some of your interests
- Shares toys, ideas, or activities
- Is kind and thoughtful
- Is fun to be with
- Listens to what you say
- Is willing to wait her turn

Find someone in your class or neighborhood who makes you feel comfortable and who is interested in some of the same things that you are. Talk to that person and make plans

to get together. When you are getting to know each other, plan to be together for only a little while, until you learn more about each other.

For the first few times you get together, be sure to do something that you both like, such as a craft project, riding bikes, playing ball, or going to a movie. If you are going to be playing a game, work together to decide on the rules of the game before you start. Make sure you don't change them once the game begins.

Here are some other ways to be a good friend:

✳ Be flexible and try your friend's ideas some of the time. Remember that everything does not always need to be done your way.

✷ If acting impulsively (without thinking) is a problem for you, try hard to slow down and think before you act. Take a minute to look at the situation and think of two ways you could act instead. If some kids are already playing a board game and you want to join, don't sit down and interrupt their game. Stop and think about what you could do. Perhaps, you could ask to play in the next game or find something else to play with until they finish their game.

✷ Good friends are kind and considerate. Make it a habit to say something nice about the other person each time you are together. When you are thoughtful about other people, you may be surprised how often they are nice to you in return.

Some kids do better during planned group activities such as baseball, scouting, 4-H, or other youth organizations. Other kids do better playing at home with just one or two friends.

In either situation, having an adult around to supervise can keep things running smoothly. If something does go wrong, the adult is there to help you.

Discuss problems you are having with friends with your parents, counselor, or therapist. Problems may not always be your fault. Sometimes, other kids just aren't being nice. Parents, counselors, and therapists can help you deal with these kids, too. With an adult's help, you can come up with ideas and solutions. They can even help you practice ways to act differently next time.

Don't forget that any friendship can have difficult moments. Sometimes the best thing to do is say you are sorry or stop doing what hurts the other person. That's not easy for anyone, but it can be the best way to keep a friendship going!

CHAPTER 10

Keeping Your Cool

Getting upset or angry can sometimes be a normal reaction to a tough situation. These reactions may even help you to tune in to things that are not going well and need to change. But anger can become a problem if it gets out of control. It is not always easy to keep your cool, especially when you are frustrated.

Getting Your Emotions under Control

Here are five steps that you can take to help you gain better control of your emotions. You may find it helpful to work on these steps with an adult (such as a parent or counselor) until you feel comfortable trying them on your own.

STEP ONE: Find out what makes you upset or angry.

The most important step in managing your emotions is finding out what situations upset you or make you angry. Do you get upset when you are tired or someone teases you? Do you have problems whenever you are with a certain person? Do you get angry when you have to rush or feel you are not being listened to? What about when you think things are unfair? Try to make a list of when you get upset and what has caused it. These situations are sometimes called your "trigger points."

STEP TWO: Avoid your trigger points.

Once you have made the list of what bothers you the most, the next step is to find ways to avoid these trigger points. That might include not playing with a certain person or moving away when you see him or her coming. Try thinking of solutions when you are well-rested and able to think clearly. And don't be afraid to ask for help if you need it.

If it is hard for you to find a quick solution or to avoid becoming upset or angry, learn to recognize signs that you are getting angry and take steps to calm down.

Everyone has different warning signs.

STEP THREE: Recognize the early signs of anger.

In order to take action against anger, be aware of some of the early signs that you are getting upset. Once you learn to recognize these warning signs, you can make changes before it is too late. Everyone has different warning signs.

Here are some signs of anger:

- You start breathing faster or you feel like you can't catch your breath.
- Your face gets red and hot.
- You begin sweating.
- Your heart starts beating fast.
- You make fists or your muscles become tense.
- You start to cry.
- Your voice gets louder or shaky.

STEP FOUR: Take a time-out.

When you have any of these early warning signals, it's a good idea to take a time-out. By moving away from the situation, you will be better able to get back into control. (See page 50 for a discussion of time-out.)

STEP FIVE: Get back into control.

Here are several suggestions or strategies you might try to gain better control over your emotions:

- Try counting to 10 slowly.
- Take a walk. (Make sure you let someone know this is what you are doing!)

- Get a drink of water.
- Imagine that you are someplace else. Think of a place where you feel very comfortable. Then pretend you are there.
- Practice deep breathing. (You have seen athletes do this before a big shot or big play. Breathe in slowly to the count of 8, hold it for the count of 4, and then breathe out slowly to the count of 8. After doing this deep, slow breathing 3 or 4 times, you should feel calmer.)

Other Tools to Help You Feel Calm

There are other ways to feel calm, less hyperactive, and more in control. These include:

Yoga • Progressive Muscle Relaxation • Meditation

At first, you will need to practice these tools with a parent, teacher, or therapist, but soon you'll be able to use them on your own to feel calmer and more in control. Let's talk about each one.

✱ **Yoga.** You probably have heard of yoga before, but may not have known it can help kids with AD/HD. Yoga combines physical movement and postures, control of your breathing, concentration, and relaxation to help you feel more in control.

But how can yoga help? To find out the answer to this question, scientists did an experiment with a group of first, second, and third grade kids with AD/HD who practiced yoga by watching a video tape, *Yoga Fitness for Kids,* with a teacher and other kids. They did this during the school day for 30 minutes, twice a week for 3 weeks. During the weeks when the kids were practicing yoga, the kids with AD/HD were able to focus in the classroom for the same amount of time as their classmates without AD/HD. When they stopped doing the yoga, they were still on task more than they had been before they ever started the program, but not as much as when they went to yoga sessions. These results are interesting and show that yoga might help kids with AD/HD pay attention better. You may want to try yoga and see if it helps you!

> Relaxing your body is a great way to help get rid of stress, calm yourself, and quiet your mind.

✳ **Progressive Muscle Relaxation.** Relaxing your body is a great way to help get rid of stress, calm yourself when you are angry, and quiet your mind. If you have trouble settling down during the day or falling asleep at night, try the following exercise to relax your body. By tightening and relaxing the muscles in every part of your body, you can release stress and feel calmer.

You can relax any time you want by following these steps:

1. Start by lying down on your back, on your bed or the floor, with your eyes closed.

2. Tense (tighten) the muscles in your toes and feet as hard as you can by curling your toes under.

3. Hold this tightening while counting to 10 slowly.

4. Then release and relax these muscles. Lie quietly for one or two minutes.

5. Next tense your calves (backs of your lower legs) by pointing your toes while counting to 10.

6. Relax for a few minutes.

7. Now tense or tighten the muscles in your legs while counting to 10.

8. Relax and lie quietly for a few minutes.

9. Now tighten the muscles in your stomach while counting to 10.

10. Relax on your back for one or two minutes.

11. Continue this tightening and relaxing with all the muscle groups in your hands, arms, shoulders, neck, and face.

After tensing each group of muscles, hold the tightness to the count of ten. Then relax the muscle group for a few minutes.

When you are finished with this exercise, lie quietly with your eyes closed and breathe slowly in and out for awhile. Listen to your breathing and hold on to this relaxed feeling.

✳ **Meditation.** Meditation combines breathing and relaxation to help you clear your mind of all other thoughts by helping you focus on your breathing. It can be very helpful, especially when you are stressed or feeling out of control. Your AD/HD may make it more difficult to clear your mind, since many thoughts keep jumping in. Meditation can be difficult for many  people to learn, so don't get frustrated if it takes time for you.

Meditation can be done sitting, walking, or lying down.

Here is one way to meditate.

1. Begin by sitting or lying comfortably on the floor or on a pillow.

2. Place your hands in your lap or at your sides.

3. Close your eyes.

4. Breathe in and out slowly and evenly.

5. Breathe in and count one.

6. Breathe out to the count of two.

7. Keep doing this until you reach 20.

8. After you get to 20, keep breathing slowly and try to be very still. Think about things that make you happy, or just let your mind wander.

9. After a few minutes, take a deep breath in and out to end the meditation.

10. Next, stand up and stretch, feeling relaxed and calm.

It may take some time before you can do this exercise alone. If you want to learn meditation, you can work with someone who teaches these techniques or look at the Resources at the end of this book for a useful website and guided meditation CD.

CHAPTER 11

Staying Focused

Staying focused is difficult for lots of kids. It can be especially hard for kids with AD/HD. Fortunately, there are many ways you can improve your concentration. Try some of these tips when you are finding it hard to pay attention. Make sure you tell your teacher or parent ahead of time, so that they will know what you are doing (and why this activity is helpful for you).

- Fidgeting sometimes helps improve your focus. When you fidget, you move parts of your body, such as your fingers or toes. Try fidgeting in ways that will not bother other people but will let you move around somewhat. Some kids use a "fidget object," such as a piece of clay or a squeeze ball.

- Try doodling or drawing with a pencil or marker while you are listening. This works only when you really can listen and draw at the same time.

- Use different kinds of pens and pencils or different colors to make doing your work more interesting.

⦿ Keep a water bottle nearby and take sips while you are working or listening.

Having trouble focusing while doing your homework? Here are some more ideas for you to try:

⦿ Listen to music. Sometimes working with music in the background can be helpful. Different kinds of music work well for different people, so explore what is best for you.

⦿ Give yourself breaks. Work hard for a period of time (such as 15 or 20 minutes), then run around outside or do some exercise for a few minutes. Go back to work for another 15 minutes, then take another short break. You may find that you work better this way.

⦿ Use a clock or timer so that you can keep track of time.

⦿ Pet your dog or cat. If you have a dog or cat at home, pet it while you study. This is a nice way to get a little movement, and your pet will love you for it!

⦿ Move. Try moving around while you study and see if it works for you. You can use a rocking chair, pedal an exercise bicycle, or jump rope while you are trying to memorize or study something.

Exercising

Have you ever noticed how you feel calmer and more focused after P.E. class or playing sports? Getting regular exercise is important for good health and may help increase your attention. How do you usually spend your free time? If you spend a lot of time watching television or playing computer or video games, your body and brain may not be getting the exercise they really need.

There are lots of ways to make exercise a fun part of your life. What physical activities do you enjoy? There are plenty to choose from! Playing outside with friends, riding a bike, swimming, dancing, or martial arts are a few that a lot of kids like. They all give your body a great workout. Organized team sports, such as soccer or softball, are good, too! Talk with your parents and work out an activity schedule that will be fun and easy to follow. Plan activities to make sure you get enough exercise during the busy school year.

So get out of that chair or off the couch! Move around, feel good and watch how your ability to concentrate improves, too.

Playing Sports

Some kids with AD/HD enjoy playing team sports. If you are on a team, talk with your parents and the coach to see how they can help you play your best and avoid problems. If team sports are not for you, consider other sports where the goal is to improve your own performance, such as swimming, diving, ice skating, or martial arts.

Getting Outdoors

Experts have found that spending time outdoors in "green space" can help improve some symptoms of AD/HD. Green space is any area that has trees and grass, like parks and most backyards. After spending time in green spaces, kids are less hyperactive and may improve their ability to focus. Because there are so many things to do outdoors (searching for nature items, playing a game, or even reading a book), this is a good way to do something positive for yourself while having fun!

Going to Camp

Camp gives you an opportunity to get outdoors and be active. To make sure you have a good time at camp, use some of the same techniques that work for you during the school year. At camp, you need to follow directions, manage a schedule and keep your things organized. If you take medication during the year, discuss with your parents and doctor whether you should also be taking it at camp. Taking your medication may make camp a more positive experience for you. Many pediatricians recommend that kids with AD/HD take their medication at camp to make sure that they have fun, get along with others, and play safely.

CHAPTER 12

Improving Study and Organization Skills

There are many things you can do to become more in control of your life, both at home and at school. Here are some of the concerns kids with AD/HD often have:

- How can I become better at following directions?
- How can I be a better listener?
- How can I get better organized and not lose things?
- How can I keep track of all the things I need to do?
- How can I get my work done on time?
- How can I stop being so messy?
- How should I study for tests?
- How can I get better grades?

We'll answer these questions in the following sections.

Following Directions

If it is hard for you to remember everything your teacher tells you, try writing a few **key words** while the teacher is speaking. For example, your teacher is telling you about tomorrow's assignment. She says, "The work must be written in cursive. It should be at least two paragraphs long. Be sure to use correct quotation marks." You can jot down a few reminder notes to look at when you get home. The notes might look like this:

(✱) Tomorrow's Assignment
1. cursive
2. two paragraphs
3. use quotation marks

Let's try another one. Your math teacher says, "Open to page 39 in your book. Do section B in class now and section C tonight for homework. Remember to use pencil and graph paper." Your notes might look like this:

→ Math Homework
1. page 39
2. section C
3. graph paper

If it is difficult for you to write notes, try making a few quick pictures to help you remember something. Your mother says, "After dinner, feed the dog. Then clean up your desk."

Here is another one. Your P.E. teacher says, "Bring in your sneakers and shorts for P.E. tomorrow."

You may need to remind adults (such as parents, teachers, and sports coaches) that it is hard for you to remember a lot of information when you are only hearing it. Perhaps teachers or a classmate can write the information down for you. Work out an arrangement with your teacher to find someone in your classes who is a fast note-taker and would be willing to help you.

Many students use portable word processors, such as Alpha-Smarts, Quick Pads, or laptop computers, at school. This is really helpful if your handwriting is hard to read or if you write slowly. Taking notes, writing reminders, and keeping track of what you need to do is much easier if you write it and store the information on your computer or phone.

Managing Your Time

If you have trouble keeping track of time, use clocks, timers, and calendars to help. Before you start a task, guess how long it will take to complete. Then time yourself and compare this time with your guess. With practice, you will get better at figuring out how long things take. You can keep a record of your progress on a piece of paper or the computer.

PROJECT	AMOUNT OF TIME	
	GUESS	ACTUAL
1. Math homework	40 minutes	20 minutes
2. Check book report	10 minutes	30 minutes
3. Check Spelling sentences	45 minutes	40 minutes
4. Clean backpack	2 minutes	20 minutes

Try using a timer or an alarm when you have only a certain amount of time to do something. This can help you stay focused and might keep you from getting sidetracked. If you have a watch with an alarm or a personal timer, set it to go off at the time you want to be finished, or set it a few minutes before you need to stop. These kinds of watches also work well to remind you when you need to do something, such as go to the nurse's office for medicine or take your dog for her afternoon walk.

When you have lots of different things to do, it usually helps to make a list. Here are some examples of different kinds of lists that might come in handy.

★Things to DO TODAY!!
 1. Get permission slip signed.
 2. Study for spelling test.
 3. Practice part for the play. ☺
 4. Do two pages in language work book.
 5. Clean hamster cage.

Make sure to write down when an assignment or project is due. This is called a **due date.** Once you have written down due dates, you will not have to worry about remembering them in your head. Keep this information in a place where you can check it every day. Some kids like to use large wall calendars to record due dates. You can also set a reminder alarm on the calendar on your cell phone or email, or the calendar on your computer. Make sure to enter all your assignments, tests, and projects, to keep track of what to do and when things are due.

When you have a large assignment, such as a research report, a big test, or a science fair project coming up, break down the assignment into smaller steps. Then write each of these steps on a separate day of the calendar so you will know what to do on each day. Some examples might be:

SUNDAY	MONDAY	TUESDAY	WEDNESDAY	THURSDAY	FRIDAY	SATURDAY
		1	2	3 Read Chapter 4 of biography	4	5 make list of items needed for science fair project
6 Read chapter 5 of biography	7	8 work on science fair project 25 minutes	9	10 work on science fair project 25 minutes	11	12
13	14 Read last chapter of biography	15	16 write notes about biography	17	18 Make an outline for biography written report	19
20	21	22	23	24	25	26

Try to spread out what you have to do so that no day becomes overloaded. At first, it may be helpful to have a parent, teacher, tutor, or counselor work with you to show you how to break big jobs into smaller parts.

Some students make running reminder lists on the computer, so they can add or take away items easily. Wipe-off boards and blackboards are easy to use, since you can erase things as they are completed, and add others that you need to remember.

Small electronic devices that fit in your pocket or backpack are great for storing lots of information: due dates, test dates, assignments, reminders, and special events. Since they are expensive and easy to lose, work out with your parents when they will be ready to let you own one.

Here is something important to remember about managing time. Things often take longer to do than we think they will, and unexpected things can happen (a relative comes to visit or you get sick) and change your original plan. So it's a good idea to build extra time into your plans. If you think something you've never done before is going to take 15 minutes, allow yourself 30 minutes. Or when planning a big assignment, plan to finish a few days early in case you need extra time toward the end.

Managing Your Homework

Homework assignment books can help you keep up with your work if you use them each day. Make sure to write down all your assignments. Don't rely on your memory. If there is no assignment in a subject that day, write in "none," so it doesn't look like you forgot to write something down.

> Things often take longer to do than we think they will.

Check your assignment book each day before leaving school, so you know what you will need to bring home that day. When you get home, review your assignment book and make a homework plan. A parent, homework helper, or babysitter can help you go over what you need to do that night.

If your school requires you to use a special assignment book, learn how to use it at the beginning of the year. If the spaces in the book are small, decide where you will write additional homework notes and reminders to yourself. If you are allowed to choose your own assignment book, you and a parent should look for one that is well organized and gives you plenty of room to write. As you complete something, cross it off your list. If you need to continue working on something, you can move it to another date.

Some schools now have homework hotlines or teacher websites, so you can call in or log on to check what your assignments are.

If you need help understanding an assignment or just want more information, there are many websites that help students. Some of them are run through your public library, so that is a good place to start looking. Work with your parents and teachers to find the most useful websites when you need extra homework help.

Organize Your Things

If you have a messy bedroom, school desk, locker, or backpack, work with an adult to develop a better system. You may also want to try one or more of the following ideas:

- Some kids with AD/HD find it useful to put shelves in their bedroom closet or on their wall. Each shelf can be marked with the name of a particular item or group of items. Using plastic baskets can also help you organize things.

- Colors can make organizing easier. For example, you might put all math work in a red folder and history in a green folder. At home, you might put underwear in a drawer with a yellow sticker, shirts in a drawer with a blue sticker, and socks in a drawer with a red sticker. Choose a specific day and time each week for cleaning out your backpack or desk. You might want an adult to help you with this, too.

- Try keeping a box near the front door of your home or in a special spot in the bedroom or family room. You can use the box for schoolbooks when you come home.

Colors can make organizing easier.

Take the books out to do homework and put them back when you are finished. You can also put in anything you need for school the next day, such as your clothes for P.E or a permission slip for a class trip. Everything will be in one place when you leave in the morning.

- Pack for school the night before to avoid rushing in the morning. You will be less likely to forget the things that you need.

Getting more organized will make your days run more smoothly and help your confidence grow.

> Getting more organized will make your days run more smoothly.

Improving Study Habits

There are many different ways to study. Some kids learn better when they review or discuss material with a friend, parent, or tutor. This gives these students a chance to repeat information and remember it better. It also allows them to ask questions if there is something they are not sure about.

Another study strategy is to underline or highlight the most important information to study. This helps you focus on only the important material, instead of paying attention to the less important information.

Some students study using an audio recorder. They read aloud the most important points from notes or the book. They later listen to the recorded notes over and over. This works well for kids who need to hear things several times in order to really learn them. Also, when you speak into the recorder, you are saying the information in a way that makes sense to you, so you'll be more likely to remember it later.

Students who get restless sometimes like moving around while studying. This helps get rid of extra energy and makes it easier to concentrate. Try walking as you read or pedal an exercise bicycle, if you have one. Try exercising before studying. This may help you feel more relaxed when you have to sit down and get started.

If your teacher gives you a study guide, make sure to use it when you prepare for a test. It lets you know what your teacher thinks is important. You can also make up your own study guide or work with a classmate to make one together.

Kids who have trouble concentrating sometimes need to find a quiet study place that has very few distractions. Think of a place where you can focus best and try to study there.

When you need to concentrate, be sure to take regular short breaks, so that you don't start to feel sleepy or bored. Walk around, play a short game of catch, or go get a healthy snack. The change and movement will help you get back to work with better focus.

Try studying in different places or positions. Some kids like listening to music when they study. Try different ways to study, even those you never used before. This may help you figure out what works best for you. Some kids have many ways that they study best. Other kids find that one way or one place works well for them. Get to know what works for you, and experiment with some new strategies every once in a while. As you get older, you may discover some other techniques work well.

Try different ways to study, even those you never used before.

Improving Schoolwork

In order to improve schoolwork, first make sure that you are paying attention. To decrease distractions, some kids with AD/HD sit near the front of the classroom or near the teacher. Some kids stay focused on their work by having the teacher give them a pre-arranged secret signal to remind them to get back on track. These signals include having the teacher tap her desk or hold a special pencil or say a "signal" word.

(If the teacher agrees to help you stay on track in this way, you should work together and come up with your own signal.)

Before you start your work, read all the directions at least two times. This way, you will make sure to do the right thing from the start.

Check over your classwork and homework. You want your teachers to see how much you really know, so show them work without careless errors.

Doing work on the computer makes it look better, and it is much easier to correct your mistakes. Remember to always back up your work on the computer so you don't lose it.

Improving Proofreading

Proofreading means checking over your work for mistakes. Look for mistakes in spelling, punctuation, and capitalization. Although proofreading doesn't seem like much fun, it is the best way to find mistakes and turn in work that you can feel proud of.

- Check to see if all your sentences are complete and make sense. Read what you wrote out loud to see if the sentences say what you meant to say.

- Read your paper from the bottom up. This may help you spot spelling and punctuation errors more easily.

- Make a game of it. See how many mistakes you can find in five minutes. Exchange papers with a friend and look for errors in each other's work.

- Use the computer for longer homework assignments. It is easier to spot mistakes.

- Use the **spell-check** program on your computer. You can also buy a small portable spell-check device to use in school.

Organizing Your Ideas

Some kids with AD/HD have lots of good ideas, but find it hard to organize their thoughts when writing. Using graphic organizers, such as webs or outlines, is a good way to set up your ideas before you start writing. Jotting down your ideas and organizing them into categories will give you an order to follow when you begin to write. Some graphic organizers have different sections for you to fill with your ideas. Then, you can use the organizer as your guide once you begin to write. Your teacher may give you some examples of graphic organizers to try. There is also software for graphic organizers, as well as plenty of sample graphic organizers online.

Improving Test Results

To improve the grades you get on tests, make sure that you have enough time to study. Studying for tests over many days makes it is easier to review all the material and makes you less worried. Then, when you begin the test, take a deep breath and remind yourself that you are prepared!

Don't pick up that pencil to start the test until you have read all of the directions at least twice. During the test, check the clock a few times (or bring a watch) so that you make sure you are using your time well.

Keep a few pieces of clean paper on your desk when you take a test. If you find it hard to remember information, use the blank paper to jot down everything that comes into your head about the subject. This is a trick that may help you recall the material you have studied.

When you take an essay test, write notes on the paper, reminding yourself what you want to be sure to include in your answer. You can also write a quick outline or web with your ideas and follow it when you write your essay. You can look back and not worry about forgetting an important point.

Check over test paper completely before you hand it in. Wait a few minutes and then check it again.

When you get your graded test back, take some time to look it over. See what you did well and what you need to improve next time. Talk it over with a parent, teacher, or tutor who can help you figure out how to better prepare for a test the next time.

CHAPTER 13

Learning about
Medications for AD/HD

For some kids with AD/HD, a doctor may prescribe a **stimulant medication** to help with attention problems. Stimulants are drugs that increase focus and attention. Stimulants can also reduce impulsivity or hyperactivity, by "turning on the brakes" in the brain.

Unlike with other medicines, doctors prescribe stimulants to improve the way the brain works, not to fix someone who is sick.

Here are some of the things that kids have said about taking medication to treat their AD/HD:

What You Need to Know

If your doctor has **prescribed** medicine for your AD/HD, you should learn as much as you can about it, including its name, what it looks like, and the **dose** (amount) you are supposed to take each time. This is all very important information.

Never take medicine when you don't know what it is. Only take medicine from someone who is allowed to give it to you, such as your parent, babysitter, or the school nurse. Don't take anyone else's medication, ever. Never share your medicine with anyone else, even if they have the same problems paying attention that you have.

Medication Is Only One Part of AD/HD Treatment

Medications can be very helpful if you have AD/HD. But the medication can't do everything. If you have problems with schoolwork, organization, or getting along with others, you still need to learn other ways to improve. Members of your team are there to help you. For example, medication may help you improve your concentration, but to do better in school you may need to spend extra time with your teacher or tutor to learn good study skills. You still need to study and do all of your assignments, but you may find that schoolwork will go more smoothly once you are more organized and better focused.

The Right Medication for You

AD/HD affects your life. All day. Every day. While some kids may only need medication during the school day, others may also need medication later in the day for homework, after-school activities, and getting along at home.

Today, there are many medications to treat AD/HD. With so many medications available, you, your parents, and your doctor have lots of choices. Each child with AD/HD is unique. That means that certain medications are better at reducing symptoms for some kids than for others. You and your parents will work with your doctor to figure out which type of medicine is best for you. Sometimes it may take a while to find the right medication and amount to help you do better in school, at home, and with friends. So don't get discouraged if your doctor has you try a few medicines before you find the one that's right for you.

> Certain medications are better at reducing symptoms for some kids than for others.

Medications to Treat AD/HD

Stimulants are the most common medications used to treat AD/HD. Stimulants are medicines that increase attention and concentration by changing the levels of the neurotransmitters in the brain and making the brain's

receptors work more efficiently. (See Chapter 4 for a review of what's going on in your brain.) This makes focusing and learning easier. Stimulants can also decrease impulsivity and help you manage your behavior. Then you may have an easier time following the rules and doing what you know is right. Stimulants have been used to treat AD/HD for a long time. Over the years, many hundreds of **research studies** have been done to prove that stimulant medications to treat AD/HD are safe when used correctly.

Medications prescribed for treating AD/HD come in different forms that last for different lengths of time. Doctors call these short-, intermediate-, and long-acting medications, depending on how long a pill or patch works. Your doctor and your parents, with input from you and your teachers, will decide which medicine is right for you.

Short-acting Medications

These medications usually start working about 20 minutes after you take them, and last about 4 hours. If you take these pills before school or early in the morning, they will usually wear off by lunch. The doctor might then recommend another pill at lunchtime at school. Some kids need a third dose (amount) of medication to help attention during homework and other after-school activities. The most commonly used brands of the short-acting (lasts a few hours) medicines are Ritalin, Dexedrine, and Adderall. These are all stimulants.

Intermediate-acting Medications

These pills last a little longer (up to 6 hours) and often allow kids to get through the entire school day with only one pill in the morning. If that pill wears off after school, a short-acting pill may help for after-school activities or homework. The intermediate-acting forms of these medications are also stimulants. They are Ritalin SR, Metadate CD, and Focalin.

Long-acting Medications

The effects of long-acting medications usually last for 10 to 12 hours. With each of these medicines, kids take only one pill or patch in the morning and its effects usually last into the evening. Long-acting stimulant pills used to treat AD/HD are named Concerta, Focalin XR, Vyvanse, and Adderall XR. Skin patches from the pharmacy are a newer way to give a stimulant for

AD/HD. This patch is called Daytrana. Once the patch is stuck on, like a band-aid, it gives your medicine for AD/HD through your skin. Kids can wear this patch for 9 hours, but the medicine's effect lasts for about 10 hours total. You can also wear the patch for less time if you are not doing as many activities during the day. You can put it on later if you sleep later in the morning or need to stay up and pay attention later at night or for a special event.

> Sometimes medicines make people who take them feel uncomfortable in some way.

There are also long-acting medications that are **non-stimulants** (not stimulants). These non-stimulants act a little differently in the brain, but still help control AD/HD throughout the day. Newer versions of the non-stimulants are Strattera, Intuniv, and Kapvay.

Each year new medications are being made. Some work better and last longer. AD/HD cannot be cured, but it can be controlled. Medication can help. Over time, your AD/HD may improve, but it is important to continue to work with your doctor so that you receive the best treatment to keep your symptoms under good control.

Side Effects

Sometimes medicines make people who take them feel uncomfortable in some way. These problems are known as

side effects. Some of the medicines used to treat AD/HD make some people feel less hungry. This doesn't happen to everyone, but if it happens to you, it is important that you not lose weight. Eat a good breakfast, and try to eat

something at lunchtime. You can also make up for lost calories by eating nutritious snacks in the afternoon and before you go to bed at night.

A few kids complain about a stomachache after they take the medicine. Be sure to tell your parents, doctor, or teacher if you have that problem. Eating some crackers or drinking a glass of water will usually make the feeling go away. You can also try drinking a full glass of water when taking the pill, instead of just a sip. That may prevent the stomachache from happening in the first place.

You should avoid citrus drinks or fruits (orange, grapefruit, lemon, or lime) when you take some stimulant medicines because they can reduce the effectiveness of the medicine. You can take most of the stimulant medications before or after you eat.

Working with Your Doctor

Remember to tell your parents and doctor how the medicine you take makes you feel, so they can help you. Visit your doctor and have a check-up regularly while you are taking your medicine. Your doctor can check your height, weight, and **blood pressure,** and do blood tests, if needed, to make sure you are healthy and growing.

Your doctor is the person in charge of your medicine. By following your progress closely, he or she will be able to decide how much medicine you need and when you should take it. Your doctor will adjust the dose (amount) or change the medication until you find the best one for you. When you visit your doctor, let him or her know how the medicine works for you. Talk about any changes you have noticed. Make sure all of your opinions and questions are heard and answered.

CHAPTER 14

Taking Care of Yourself

Taking good care of yourself includes getting enough sleep, eating healthy foods, staying safe, and feeling good about yourself. This may mean a little extra work, but it will be worth it.

Getting Enough Sleep

Getting enough sleep helps you feel more alert and focused the next day. Sometimes kids with AD/HD have trouble falling asleep or getting enough sleep at night. This can make them **irritable** and less attentive the next day. If you have difficulty falling asleep, try the following tips:

- Listen to quiet music.
- Try progressive relaxation or meditation, described on pages 59–62.
- Make sure your room is dark so things you see do not distract you.
- Don't play video games or do homework right before getting into bed.
- Take a relaxing bath in the evening.
- Pack your backpack and set out your clothes before

you get into bed so you don't have to worry about them.

- Get enough exercise during the day, but not right before bedtime.
- No rough or exciting play right before bedtime. Getting too excited makes it more difficult to settle down.
- Have a small snack earlier in the evening, so you won't be hungry when you're trying to fall asleep. But be careful what you eat. A snack with lots of sugar or caffeine, like cola or chocolate, may keep you awake.

If you still have problems falling asleep after trying some of these ideas, you and your parents should talk to your doctor about it.

Eating Right

Eating a balanced diet helps you grow and have enough energy to learn and play. Some kids who take medication for their AD/HD might have less of an appetite during the day. If this happens to you, make sure to choose foods that provide good nutrition. Stay

away from unhealthy foods like sugary or fatty junk food. Eat healthful foods throughout the day to keep up your energy and to help you grow. Here's another idea if you're not usually hungry for lunch. Eat a healthy breakfast (like fruit, waffles, eggs, yogurt, cereal, and toast) and a smaller lunch (half a sandwich, a chicken leg with carrot sticks, or yogurt and fruit). Have a large afternoon snack (pasta, a hamburger, or soup and crackers) or an early dinner when your appetite returns.

These foods are only suggestions. Your doctor or a nutritionist can give you more ideas. Work with your parents so that they can have your favorite healthy foods in the house. Kids with AD/HD should avoid foods that have too many artificial ingredients, like food colorings and preservatives, because those may make hyperactive behaviors worse.

Staying Safe

When kids with AD/HD act impulsively or don't take time to think about what they are doing, they may have more accidents or get into trouble more often. To stay safe, it helps to:

- Be with friends who know how to play safely.
- Review safety rules with your parents.

- If you are allowed to cross the street by yourself, cross at the corner and only after you have checked for cars coming from both directions
- Play where an adult is nearby to supervise.
- Make believe your parent or teacher is standing right next to you. What would he or she tell you to do?
- If someone would describe an activity as dangerous, don't do it.

Feeling Good about Yourself

If you have a difficult day, or your parents complain about your behavior, or say that you don't listen to directions, you may start feeling badly about yourself. At these times, remind yourself that you have *lots* to be proud of and that you are good at many things. Try to remember your many good qualities. Sometimes, making a list (either in your head or on paper) of nice things that have happened can improve the way you feel.

Things I'm GOOD At

1. _____
2. _____
3. _____
4. _____
5. _____

NICE Things That Have Happened to Me

1. _____
2. _____
3. _____
4. _____
5. _____

Afterword

To Boys and Girls with AD/HD

You have taken a big step by reading this book and learning about AD/HD. We hope you now know more about taking control of your life and about how to put on the brakes.

Use this knowledge to make positive changes in your life. Remember, AD/HD will not stop you from doing the things you really want to do. If you work hard and believe in yourself, you can succeed.

Feel free to reread any section of this book. With each reading, you will find ideas that can make your life easier. Although the suggestions in this book may seem like extra work, they are worth trying to make things better at home and at school.

Encourage the people in your life (your family, teachers, friends, and classmates) to read this book and to learn more about AD/HD and you. Try not to be afraid to ask for help when you need it. There are many people who are willing to help you.

Talk to your parents, teachers, doctor, and therapist to learn more about AD/HD and how it affects you. Work with them as you try ideas from this book. Together you may come up with other suggestions. You really can change and make improvements. Be creative! See what works for you and use it!

Your AD/HD is just one part of you. Try hard to manage it, and you will have plenty of energy left over to enjoy the many other parts of your life.

Best wishes,
Patricia O. Quinn, MD
Judith M. Stern, MA

Glossary

A

AD/HD Coach. A person who helps children or adults with AD/HD set goals, get better organized, and use their time well.

Attention Deficit Disorder (ADD). A set of problems that includes difficulty paying attention and focusing. It also includes increased distractibility.

Attention Deficit Hyperactivity Disorder (ADHD). A set of problems that includes short attention span, distractibility, impulsivity, and hyperactivity.

Attention Deficit/Hyperactivity Disorder (AD/HD). A term referring to both ADD and ADHD.

B

Blood Pressure. The pressure of the blood against the inner walls of the blood vessels. It can be measured by a cuff placed around the upper arm.

Brain. The major organ of the nervous system. It controls all mental and physical activities.

Brain Stem. A part of the brain that controls automatic functions such as breathing, heart rate, and blood pressure.

C

Cerebellum. A part of the brain that controls the movements of the muscles, helps with balance, and controls attention.

Cerebral Cortex. The outermost layer of the brain. Its networks are important for higher thinking activities such as memory and organizing information. It makes up 40 perent of total brain weight.

Combined Type. A type of attention disorder where a person has difficulty with keeping still when he needs to (hyperactivity) and who frequently acts before he thinks things through (impulsivity) as well as difficulty paying attention (inattention) and staying focused (distractibility).

Concentrate. To pay attention.

Counselor. A professional who works with kids or adults to help them understand feelings and solve problems. Counselors may work in schools or have offices in other places.

D

Disorganized or **Disorganization.** Difficulty keeping track of materials or time or both. Kids with AD/HD can be **disorganized.**

Distractibility. Trouble staying focused on just one thing.

Dose. The correct amount of medicine a person needs to take at one time for the medicine to work properly.

Due Date. The date on which an assignment or project needs to be handed in.

E

Evaluates or **Evaluation.** Testing to determine how someone is doing in school, how he or she is feeling, or to find out if a person has a problem in one or more areas.

H

Hyperactive/Impulsive Type. A type of attention disorder where the person has difficulty with keeping still when he needs to (hyperactivity) and who frequently acts before he thinks things through (impulsivity).

Hyperactivity. Excess motor activity or purposeless body movements that are greater than normally seen at a certain age. If you are **hyperactive,** it may be difficult for you to keep still.

I

Impulsive behavior or **Impulsivity.** Acting or speaking without thinking.

Inattentive Type. A type of attention disorder where the person mainly has difficulty paying attention (inattention) and staying focused (distractibility).

Inherited. Passed down from generation to generation in a family.

Irritable. Overly sensitive or in a bad mood.

K

Key Words. The most important words, such as a few words you would use to identify an assignment or remind yourself to do something.

L

Learning Difficulties. Difficulties in reading and writing assignments or learning math as well as other students seem to be able to do.

Learning Disabilities. Significant difficulties in learning to read, write, or do mathematics that cause problems in school achievement.

Learning Specialist. A teacher who has special training in working with students who have learning difficulties.

M

Medication. Substances used to treat illnesses or to improve functioning of the body or brain.

N

Neurologist. A medical doctor who is a specialist in the way the nervous system works. The nervous system of the body is made up of the brain, spinal cord, and nerves.

Neuron. A single brain cell.

Neurotransmitters. Chemical substances produced by brain cells (neurons) that act as messengers. They cross the space (synapse) between cells and carry information to other brain cells.

Non-Stimulant Medication. Medication used to treat AD/HD. This kind of medication acts differently than stimulants on the chemicals in the brain, but still improves attention and focus.

O

Organized. Able to put things in their correct order or place.

P

Pediatrician. A medical doctor who is a specialist in the health of kids and adolescents.

Prescribe. To write directions for the preparation and use of a medicine.

Professional. A person with special training and a university degree or license in a particular area.

Proofreading. Checking over written work for errors in spelling, punctuation, capitalization, and grammar.

Psychiatrist. A medical doctor who specializes in helping people who are having difficulties with their feelings or behaviors. This doctor can also prescribe medication.

Psychologist. A doctor who talks with people to help them understand their thoughts, feelings, and behaviors. Some psychologists also do testing to learn more about people so they can help them.

R

Receptors. Sites on a brain cell (neuron) that receive messages in the form of neurotransmitters from other brain cells.

Relay System. A system in the subcortex of the brain that coordinates information coming in from the brain stem and sends it to the cerebral cortex and other parts of the brain.

Research Studies. Experiments conducted by scientists to learn about what causes certain conditions and what works best to make these conditions better.

Resource Teacher. A special education teacher who works with kids individually or in small groups. Some schools call them Learning Specialists.

Scans. Special pictures taken of the brain.

Side Effects. Uncomfortable reactions that are sometimes caused by medicine.

Social Worker. A professional who works with kids and their families to help them solve their problems.

Spell-Check. A program for the computer or a small, hand-held machine that is used to find and correct spelling mistakes.

Stimulant Medication. A type of drug that increases attention and focus. Stimulants commonly used to treat AD/HD include Ritalin, Dexedrine, Concerta, Daytrana, Focalin, Adderall, Metadate, and Vyvanse.

Stressful. Something that makes a person feel tense or uncomfortable.

Subcortex. The area of the brain below and surrounded by the cerebral cortex.

Synapse. An extremely small space between two brain cells (neurons) that can be seen only with a microscope. Neurons send messages to each other across synapses.

T

Therapist. A professional who works with kids or adults to solve problems, understand feelings, or change behavior. A therapist can be a psychologist, counselor, social worker, or psychiatrist.

Transporter System. A system of proteins in the brain that carry chemicals across the cell membranes. When a brain cell (neuron) releases a neurotransmitter (messenger) into a synapse (space), the transporter system is responsible for taking the neurotransmitter back into the cell that released it.

Tutor. A person who works with kids outside of class to help them do better in school. A tutor may help with a subject area, such as reading, writing, and math, or may help with learning in general. Tutors can also help kids improve their organization and study skills.

Resources for Kids and Parents

✴ Books for Kids

● To Learn More About AD/HD

Attention, Girls! by Patricia Quinn (Magination Press)

Help Is on the Way: A Child's Book About ADD
by Jane Annunziata and Marc Nemiroff (Magination Press)

Learning to Slow Down and Pay Attention, Third Edition
by Kathleen Nadeau and Ellen Dixon (Magination Press)

The Survival Guide for Kids with ADD or ADHD
by John Taylor (Free Spirit Press)

● To Read about Kids with AD/HD

The Adventures of Phoebe Flower: Stories about a Girl with ADHD
by Barbara Roberts (Advantage Books)

Eagle Eyes: A Child's Guide to Paying Attention (Revised Edition)
by Jeanne Gehret (Verbal Images Press)

Ethan Has Too Much Energy: An Emotional Literacy Book
by Lawrence Shapiro (Boulden Publishing)

Joey Pigza Swallowed a Key
by Jack Gantos (HarperTrophy)

Otto Learns about His Medicine: A Story about Medication for Children with ADHD, Third Edition
by Matthew Galvin (Magination Press)

Sparky's Excellent Misadventures: My ADD Journal, By Me (Sparky)
by Phyllis Carpenter and Marti Ford (Magination Press)

● Books for School and Homework Help

Annie's Plan: Taking Charge of Schoolwork and Homework
by Jeanne Kraus (Magination Press)

Get Organized without Losing It
by Janet Fox (Free Spirit Publishing)

How to Be School Smart: Super Study Skills, Revised Edition
by Elizabeth James and Carol Barkin (Beech Tree Books)

How to Do Homework without Throwing Up
by Trevor Romain (Free Spirit Publishing)

Many Ways to Learn: A Kid's Book about LD
by Judith Stern and Uzi Ben-Ami (Magination Press)

The Survival Guide for Kids with LD (Learning Differences)
(Revised and Updated)
by Rhonda Cummings and Gary Fisher (Free Spirit Publishing)

◐ Books about Feelings and Behaviors

The Behavior Survival Guide for Kids:
How to Make Good Choices and Stay out of Trouble
by Thomas McIntyre (Free Spirit)

Chillax! How Ernie Learns to Chill Out, Relax, and
Take Charge of His Anger
by Marcella Marino Craver, MSEd, CAS (Magination Press)

What to Do When You Dread Your Bed: A Kid's Guide
to Overcoming Problems with Sleep
by Dawn Huebner (Magination Press)

*What to Do When You Grumble Too Much: A Kid's Guide
to Overcoming Negativity*
by Dawn Huebner (Magination Press)

*What to Do When You Worry Too Much: A Kid's Guide
to Overcoming Anxiety*
by Dawn Huebner (Magination Press)

*What to Do When Your Temper Flares: A Kid's Guide
to Overcoming Problems with Anger*
by Dawn Huebner (Magination Press)

☙ Games and Fun Activities Books about AD/HD
50 Activities and Games for Kids with ADD
by Patricia Quinn and Judith Stern (Magination Press)

*The "Putting on the Brakes" Activity Book for Young People with
ADD or ADIID*
by Patricia Quinn and Judith Stern (Magination Press)

◐ Resources for Yoga Meditation
Guided Meditation for Children: Journey into the Elements (CD)
by Chitra Sukhu (New Age Kids)

Meditation for All Kids
by Susan Kramer (SusanKramer.com Publishing)

Yoga Fitness for Kids Ages 7–12 (VHS)
by Leah Kalish (Living Arts/Giam)

✷ Books for Parents
*The ADD/ADHD Checklist: A Practical Reference for Parents
and Teachers, Second Edition*
by Sandra F. Rief, MA (Jossey Bass)

Homework Made Simple: Tips, Tools, and Solutions
for Stress Free Homework
by Ann Dolin, MEd (Advantage Books)

Late, Lost and Unprepared: A Parent's Guide to Helping Children
with Executive Functioning
by Joyce Cooper Kahn, PhD and Laurie Dietzel, PhD (Woodbine)

The Organized Child
by Donna Goldberg (Fireside)

Parenting Children with ADHD: 10 Lessons
That Medicine Cannot Teach
by Vincent J. Monastra, PhD (APA Books)

Ready for Take-Off: Preparing Your Teen with ADHD
or LD for College
by Theresa E. Laurie Maitland, PhD and Patricia O. Quinn, MD
(Magination Press)

Thinking Organized for Parents and Children: Helping Kids
Get Organized for Home, School and Play
by Rhona Gordon (Thinking Organized)

✳ Word Recognition Software

Blio, www.blioreader.com
Kurzweil 3000, www.kurzweiledu.com
ReadPlease, www.readplease.com

✳ Voice Recognition Software

Dragon Naturally Speaking, www.nuance.com

✱ Software for Graphic Organizers

Kidspiration® (grades K–5) by Inspiration Software, Inc.
Draft:Builder (grades 3–12) by Don Johnston Inc.

✱ Additional AD/HD Resources and Organizations Focusing on AD/HD

ADHD Aware, www.adhdaware.org and www.gogirlsclub.org

Accessible Books and Periodicals for People with Print Disabilities, www.bookshare.org

Audio books, Library of Congress, online at: www.loc.gov/nls/

Center for Girls and Women with ADHD, www.ncgiadd.org

Children and Adults with Attention Deficit Disorder (CHADD), www.chadd.org.

Organizational Tools for Students in Grades 3–12, www.successbydesign.com

Recordings for the Blind and Dyslexic, www.rfbd.org

✱ Author Contact Information

Patricia Quinn, MD, www.addvance.com

Judith Stern, MA, www.JudithSternEducationalConsultant.com

About the Authors

Patricia O. Quinn, MD, is a developmental pediatrician in Washington, DC. Dr. Quinn is a well-known international speaker and conducts workshops nationwide about AD/HD, and has authored several best-selling and groundbreaking books on AD/HD including *Attention, Girls! A Guide to Learn All About Your AD/HD* and with co-author Theresa Maitland, PhD, *Ready for Take-Off: Preparing Your Teen With ADHD or LD for College* and *On Your Own: A College Readiness Guide for Teens With ADHD/LD*. In 2000, Dr. Quinn received the CHADD Hall of Fame Award.

Judith M. Stern, MA, is a teacher and private educational consultant in Rockville, Maryland, specializing in work with children who have learning and attention problems. She is an experienced learning disabilities teacher, reading specialist, and classroom teacher. She consults with parents and teachers, and speaks nationally on subjects such as attention deficit disorder, learning problems, and children's study/organizational skills. She is the co-author of four children's books on AD/HD and LD, including with Uzi Ben-Ami, PhD, *Many Ways to Learn, Second Edition: A Kid's Guide to LD*. She is also the co-author of *The Dyslexia Checklist: A Practical Reference for Parents and Teachers*.